May There Always Be Su

MW01002616

May there always be sunshine.

May there always be blue skies.

3

May there always be children.

May there always be you.

5

May there always be stories.

May there always be music.

May there always be teachers to care for you!

May there always be sunshine.

May there always be blue skies.

May there always be children as special as you.